AMERICAN INDIAN ART AND CULTURE

The Ojibwa

MICHELLE LOMBERG

PRINCIPAL PHOTOGRAPHY BY MARILYN "ANGEL" WYNN

CHELSEA CLUBHOUSE

An Imprint of Chelsea House Publishers

A Haights Cross Communications Company

Philadelphia

This edition first published in 2004 in the United States of America by Chelsea Clubhouse, a division of Chelsea House Publishers and a subsidiary of Haights Cross Communications.

Chelsea Clubhouse
1974 Sproul Road, Suite 400
Broomall, PA 19008-0914

The Chelsea House world wide web address is www.chelseahouse.com

Library of Congress Cataloging-in-Publication Data

Lomberg, Michelle.
  The Ojibwa / Michelle Lomberg.
      v. cm. -- (American Indian art and culture)
Includes bibliographical references and index.
Contents: The people -- Ojibwa homes -- Ojibwa communities -- Ojibwa clothing -- Ojibwa food -- Tools and technology -- Ojibwa religion -- Ceremonies and celebrations -- Music and dance -- Language and storytelling -- Ojibwa art -- Ojibwa creation stories -- Studying the Ojibwa's past.
  ISBN 0-7910-7962-7 (Chelsea House) (lib. bdg. : alk. paper)
  1. Ojibwa Indians--History--Juvenile literature. 2. Ojibwa Indians--Social life and customs--Juvenile literature. [1. Ojibwa Indians.] I. Title. II. Series.
  E99.C6L65 2004
  977.004'97333--dc22
                                        2003017530
                        Printed in the United States of America
                          1 2 3 4 5 6 7 8 9 0 07 06 05 04 03

©2004 WEIGL EDUCATIONAL PUBLISHERS LIMITED

Project Coordinator Heather C. Hudak **Substantive Editor** Donald Wells **Design** Janine Vangool **Layout** Terry Paulhus **Photo Researcher** Wendy Cosh **Chelsea Clubhouse Editors** Sally Cheney and Margaret Brierton **Validator** JoAnn Douyette

Cover: Wigwam (Marilyn "Angel" Wynn), Chippewa Grass Dancer (Marilyn "Angel" Wynn), Ojibwa Food (Marilyn "Angel" Wynn, Moccasins (Marilyn "Angel" Wynn); Kit Breen: pages 10, 19L, 21T; Courtesy of Sam English: page 27; Bill Morgenstern: pages 19R, 21B, 22; Photos.com: pages 5, 13, 26, 30L, 30R; Marilyn "Angel" Wynn: pages 1, 3, 6, 7, 8, 9, 11T, 11B, 12, 14T, 14B, 15, 16, 17, 18, 20, 23, 24, 25T, 25B, 28, 29, 31.

Please note

CONTENTS

The People

The Ojibwa are known by three names. Members of this American Indian group call themselves Ojibwa when speaking with people who are not part of their nation. When European settlers pronounced the word *Ojibwa*, they said *Chippewa*. As a result, the United States government calls this group the Chippewa. The name Chippewa is used in **treaties** and other official documents. Both Chippewa and Ojibwa mean "puckered." The Ojibwa were known for the puckered seams on their moccasins. The Ojibwa call themselves *Anishinaabe*, which means "first people."

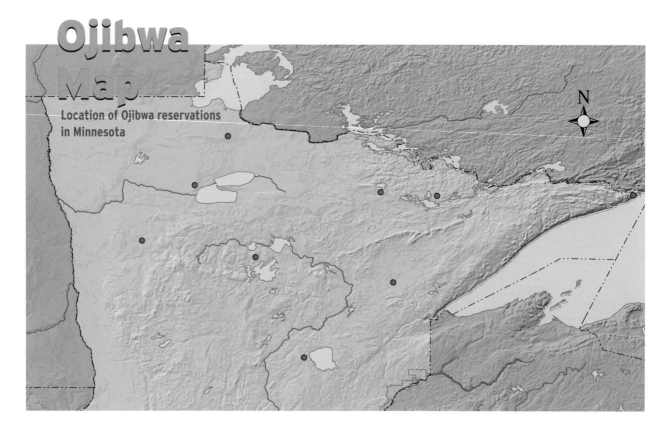

Ojibwa Map

Location of Ojibwa reservations in Minnesota

In the 1600s, the Ojibwa began trading with French fur traders. They traded beaver skins for European goods, such as guns, cloth, beads, and metal. Soon, the Ojibwa **migrated** south and west. They moved closer to trading posts and areas where beavers were abundant.

Ojibwa traditions changed in each place. The Plains Ojibwa lived in northern North Dakota and Montana. Like other American Indians living in the Plains region, these groups depended on bison hunting to survive.

The Woodlands Ojibwa included the southeastern and southwestern Ojibwa peoples. The southeastern Ojibwa lived in Michigan. They survived by hunting, fishing, and gathering. During the summer months, they also planted gardens, and harvested maple syrup and wild rice. The southwestern Ojibwa lived in Wisconsin and Minnesota. Wild rice was their main harvest. They were also gardeners, hunters, and fishermen.

Bison was the main source of food, clothing, and tools for Plains Indians.

Ojibwa Homes

Traditionally, the Ojibwa lived in structures called wigwams. A wigwam was shaped like a dome. They built wigwams from materials they found in nature. They usually used wooden poles covered with **rush mats** and birch bark.

Ojibwa men and women worked together to build wigwams. First, the men set poles in the ground. Then, they bent the poles and tied them together to make a dome-shaped frame. Next, the women covered the frame with rush mats. They laid birch-bark sheets over the mats. The birch-bark sheets overlapped like shingles on a roof. This prevented rain and wind from entering the wigwam.

Families and other members of the same clan lived in an Ojibwa village.

Wigwams kept the Ojibwa warm and dry. A fire in the center of the wigwam provided heat and light. Smoke from the fire escaped through a hole in the top of the wigwam. A blanket, animal hide, or piece of bark covered the door. The floors of the wigwam were covered with cedar bark, rush mats, or branches. People sat and slept on mats and furs. Some wigwams had low platforms that served as seats and beds.

Today, the Ojibwa live in modern buildings on **reservations** and in cities and towns. They still build traditional structures for special ceremonies.

Wigwams were easy to build and take down. They were well suited to nomadic groups.

Ojibwa Communities

Traditional Ojibwa life was loosely organized. A group of families that were related to each other was called a **clan**. Clans were named after their **totem** animals. Catfish, **Crane**, Bear, and Wolf are examples of clan names. Groups of people who were related through marriage were called **bands**. Headmen, or chiefs, led bands of 300 to 400 people. During the summer months, bands lived together in villages. In the winter, each family participated in a separate hunt.

In the winter, Ojibwa peoples lived in small family groups in the forest. In the summer, families lived in small bands near rivers and lakeshores.

Some people, such as chiefs and **shamans**, held a high position in the community. However, most people were treated as equals. Women and men worked hard throughout the year. Women grew gardens, gathered berries, and butchered meat. They made clothes from animal hides. They also fashioned

Cradleboards were thin, rectangular boards on which children were carried.

baskets and containers from bark. Men hunted and trapped big game, small animals, and birds. When necessary, the men were warriors who defended their families.

Children were an important part of Ojibwa culture. A mother would carry her baby on a cradleboard for the first year of the baby's life. Children were rarely **reprimanded**. Instead of punishment, adults used jokes or stories to teach children how to behave properly.

MODERN LIFE

Over time, there have been many changes to Ojibwa culture. In the 1800s, much of the Ojibwa's traditional hunting and gathering land was taken or bought by settlers. At that time, the U.S. government urged the Ojibwa and other American Indian groups to stop practicing their traditional ways of life. The Ojibwa were forced to end their **semi-nomadic** life and settle on reservations. Many Ojibwa left their reservations and moved to cities after World War II.

Today, many Ojibwa still practice their traditional customs. In some areas of Michigan and Wisconsin, the Ojibwa continue to hunt and gather food. Some tribes host **powwows** and other traditional celebrations. Ojibwa artists and craftspeople continue to create beautiful **artifacts** that celebrate their culture. Some students preserve their culture by studying the Ojibwa language at community colleges.

Ojibwa Clothing

Long ago, the Ojibwa made clothing from materials they found in their surroundings. Most pieces were made from **buckskin**, the **tanned** hide of a deer. Among the Ojibwa who lived around Lake Superior, the men wore leggings, moccasins, and breechcloths. Breechcloths were similar to short pants. Women wore dresses, leggings, and moccasins. In the winter, the Ojibwa wore warm fur robes and mittens. Farther south, Ojibwa women wove fiber to make shirts. The women wore these shirts under sleeveless buckskin dresses.

Traditionally, women were responsible for making clothes. They began by tanning animal hides. First, they scraped the flesh and hair from the hides. Next, they washed the hides and rubbed them with animal brains to make them soft. The hides were then smoked to give them color. Smoking also protected the hides from

Traditional clothing is still popular among the Ojibwa.

moths, which would eat holes in the hides. Women used tools made of wood and bone to cut and sew the hides. Tools called **awls** made holes in the hides. Then bone needles were used to pull thread through the holes. The thread was made of plant fiber or animal sinew, a tough strip of tissue that holds muscles to bones.

Today, many Ojibwa wear store-bought clothes. However, they still wear some traditional garments. Many people wear buckskin jackets. Colorfully beaded moccasins and mittens are also popular.

Ojibwa women added detailed decorations to the clothes they made. They used plants to make blue, green, red, and yellow dyes. They used these dyes to color porcupine quills, which were added to clothing in elaborate patterns. European traders influenced the style of Ojibwa clothes. Women were able to obtain cloth, glass beads, buttons, and ribbon from the European traders. They used these items, along with traditional materials, to make clothes.

Fur and hide from animals were used to make moccasins and mittens.

Ojibwa Food

Many Ojibwa groups ate a large variety of food. In warmer regions, Ojibwa women grew vegetables, such as beans, corn, and squash. Women and children also gathered berries. Some berries, such as blueberries and chokecherries, were dried. They ate others, such as cranberries, fresh. Raspberries were boiled to make a thick paste.

Ojibwa hunters and trappers provided their families with birds, fish, and meat. Meat was often roasted or boiled. Some meat was dried and mixed with fat and berries to make pemmican. Pemmican, which is similar to beef jerky, was a nutritious food that lasted a long time. Fish was an important food for the Ojibwa who lived around Lake Superior. Men caught fish with hooks, nets, and traps.

The Ojibwa who lived in the northeastern part of North America used water and maple sugar to make a sweet drink. Water could be flavored with other ingredients, too. Cherry twigs, wintergreen, raspberry leaves, and spruce needles were used to flavor hot and cold drinks.

Some of the foods the Ojibwa ate were beans, corn, and squash.

Wild rice was an important food for many Ojibwa. Wild rice is the seed of a grass that grows in shallow water. The Ojibwa paddled their canoes through the grass to harvest wild rice. They used sticks or paddles to knock the rice kernels into their canoes. The rice was dried, boiled, and served with meat or fowl.

The Woodlands Ojibwa collected sap from maple trees to make sugar and syrup. They ate hard sugar as a treat. They used granulated, or coarsely ground, sugar to sweeten vegetables, fruits, rice, and fish.

The Plains Ojibwa did not have wild rice or maple sugar. Their main source of meat was bison. Bison meat was often made into pemmican.

Try making this traditional Ojibwa recipe at home with an adult's help.

RECIPE

Popped Wild Rice

Ingredients:

2 to 3 tbsp. (30–44 ml) of corn oil or vegetable oil

1 cup (237 ml) of uncooked wild rice

1/4 cup (59 ml) melted butter

2 tbsp. (30 ml) of maple sugar or maple syrup

salt to taste

Equipment:

large bowl

12-inch (30-cm) skillet

1. Put the oil in the skillet.

2. With an adult's help, heat the oil on a stovetop at medium heat.

3. Add the rice to the skillet in a single layer.

4. With an adult's help, swirl the pan over the heat until most of the rice has popped.

5. Put the popped rice in a bowl.

6. Add butter, maple sugar or maple syrup, and salt to the popped rice, and enjoy.

Tools, Weapons, and Defense

The Ojibwa used materials they found in their **environment** to make tools, clothing, and shelter.

Birch bark was an especially useful material for the Woodland Ojibwa. Women used birch bark to build wigwams. They also made birch-bark bags and containers. Ojibwa men and women built birch-bark canoes, too. These canoes were strong enough to use on fast-flowing rivers. The canoes were light enough to carry between rivers and lakes.

Tools made of other materials, such as bone and wood, were also important to the Ojibwa. Men used fishing hooks and lures made of bone or wood. Women used sharpened bones to scrape hides. They used awls and needles made of bone and wood to sew clothes.

In the 1600s, the Ojibwa began using metal items. They used guns, knives, and kettles for hunting, preparing food, and warfare. They traded with the Europeans for these items.

The Ojibwa used large bark buckets to gather maple syrup.

HUNTING AND TRAVEL

Men used a variety of tools and techniques to hunt. Ojibwa hunters used blunt arrows to kill waterfowl. They caught small animals, such as rabbit, beaver, and otter, in **snares** or traps. They used larger **rawhide** snares to catch deer. Ojibwa men would also use traps made of sapling trees to trap deer. The hunter would drive the deer through the forest, into the traps.

The Ojibwa used special weapons during times of war. Ojibwa warriors often used a club. The war club was made of wood. It had a heavy, round knob on one end. Knives and bows and arrows were also used in the fighting.

The Ojibwa wore snowshoes when hunting or traveling in winter. Ojibwa snowshoes were rounded on both ends. The snowshoe frames were made of wood. Strips of animal hide were woven around the frames. This webbing allowed the wearer to walk across deep snow without sinking.

The Ojibwa made snowshoes like the ones pictured here. With these snowshoes, the Ojibwa walked over the snow without sinking through the thick powder.

Ojibwa Religion

In traditional Ojibwa religion, the world was full of spirits. The Ojibwa called these spirits *manitous*. People tried to please the spirits by praying and offering tobacco. In return, the spirits provided good weather, animals to hunt, and **bountiful** harvests. Some Ojibwa groups believed in a creator called *Kitchi Manitou*, or Great Spirit.

Sometimes, Ojibwa holy men had visions. One holy man had a vision of dancers. This vision lead to the creation of the Jingle Dance that is often performed by Ojibwa women.

The Ojibwa who lived around Lake Superior called the lake *Kitchigami*. Kitchigami was worshiped as a giver of life. Some spirits were not kind. The Ojibwa of Lake Superior feared the *Windigo*. They believed this evil spirit was a man-eating giant. Other evil or angry spirits could bring illness and famine to the Ojibwa.

Ojibwa shamans were people with spiritual power. They gained this power during vision quests. Shamans were usually older men. They used their power to cure diseases brought on by evil spirits.

The Midewiwin Society has been an important part of Ojibwa religion since the 1700s. It is also known as the Great Medicine Society. This society is devoted to curing illnesses and preserving old traditions. Members of the Midewiwin Society are leaders or healers who receive their healing power from the Creator. Medicine men and women are called the Mide. The Mide invite people who appear to have healing powers to join the society. New members are taught to use plants for healing. They also learn how to conduct religious ceremonies. Members of the Mide are expected to be honest and respect other people. Other American Indian groups, such as the Ottawa and Potawatomi, are also members of the Midewiwin Society.

Dreams were important to the Ojibwa. They believed dreams brought them wisdom. For young Ojibwa men, a dream quest was an important part of maturing. During a dream quest, young men would journey into the forest alone. They would spend several days in the forest without food. During this time, they would have a vision of their special guardian spirit. Young women also had visions, but they were not expected to participate in a dream quest.

Ojibwa Indians decorated pipes with intricate designs.

Ceremonies and Celebrations

The Ojibwa held many ceremonies and celebrations throughout the year. Springtime brought many reasons to celebrate. After spending the long winter apart, bands reunited to build summer villages. The maple sugar harvest was another holiday time. Families worked together to collect maple sap and prepare sugar.

The First Fruits ceremony took place during the wild rice harvest in late summer. The first rice grain harvested each season was offered to the Great Spirit. The rice grain was wrapped in tobacco leaves and placed in the water where it had been gathered. Then the sweet **sage** spice was burned. The smoke from the burning sage carried a message of thanks to the Great Spirit.

Many years ago, the Ojibwa celebrated the Feast of the Dead. This feast was held every year. The Feast of the Dead was a time to remember and honor those who had died during the past year. It was also an opportunity for people from different villages to gather together.

Carefully designed baskets were used to collect syrup for the maple sugar harvest.

In addition to a feast, people enjoyed dancing, games, and contests. Guests received gifts from the host village.

When they were not working in the fields, hunting, or building, the Ojibwa participated in dances, sports, and games. Lacrosse was one popular sport. Ojibwa men also enjoyed gambling games. They made dice from animal bones to play gambling games.

Powwows take place throughout the year in many Ojibwa communities.

POWWOWS

The Ojibwa continue to practice traditional celebrations. Many reservations host annual powwows. People of all ages gather at these events. They use music and games to celebrate their culture. There are competitions for dancers, drummers, and singers. Artists display traditional and modern arts and crafts. Powwows are joyful gatherings, but they are also sacred events.

Children learn about their culture by attending a powwow.

Music and Dance

Music has always been important to the Ojibwa way of life. In ancient Ojibwa culture, songs were performed on many occasions. Some songs told stories to entertain children and adults. Others helped warriors prepare for battle. Healers sang to cure illnesses. Songs were also part of religious ceremonies.

The drum is an instrument used in Ojibwa music. Drums are made from wood and animal hide. Drums represent honesty, life, and sharing. The round shape of the drum symbolizes the circle of life. Drums are always treated with great respect. The Drum Keeper is responsible for protecting the drum. He prevents people from reaching across a drum or using the drum as a table or chair. Drums are placed in the center of the dance area and surrounded by four or more singers. Dancers dance in a circle around the drums and the singers.

The Grass Dance is very graceful, with the dancer's costume resembling grass blowing on the prairie.

CEREMONIAL DANCING

Dancing is another important part of Ojibwa culture. Usually, Ojibwa men and women perform traditional dances separately. Rattles and drums are used to create Ojibwa music. The dancers keep time to the beat of the drum. Some dances tell stories about war or hunting.

The Grass Dance is one traditional Ojibwa dance. It is performed by Ojibwa men. The dancers wear clothes decorated with yarn or ribbon. These materials resemble long blades of grass. The dancers make graceful, swaying movements, to represent grass blowing in the breeze.

Today, Ojibwa people still enjoy traditional music and dances. People gather at powwows to display their song and dance skills. They compete in singing, dancing, and drumming contests.

The most colorful, fastest-moving, and most physically demanding dance is the Fancy Dance.

Ojibwa children also participate in ceremonial dancing.

Language and Storytelling

The Ojibwa call their language *Anishinaabemowin*. The Ojibwa language belongs to the Algonquian **language family**. The Ojibwa language shares similar features with more than 30 other American Indian languages. Many of these languages are no longer spoken. Schools and colleges in several Ojibwa communities keep the Ojibwa language and traditions alive. There are many **dialects** of the Ojibwa language. The following are some Ojibwa words and phrases:

Ojibwa storytellers pass on the knowledge and understanding of past generations.

Ojibwa	English
aanii	hello
Aniish na?	How are you?
Migwetch	Thank you
aki	Earth
ishkode	fire
waabooz	rabbit
mazinaatesichigan	television set
wiisini	eating
baapi	laughing
anokii	working
Nimbaap	I am laughing.
Niwiisin	I am eating.

Ojibwa families used storytelling as a form of entertainment on long winter nights. Funny stories were told to amuse young children. Other stories were about the spirit world. Ancient tales were passed down from generation to generation. Storytellers also created stories about current events.

The adventures of Nanabozho were popular subjects for stories. In Ojibwa **mythology**, Nanabozho was a hero who helped and protected people. He was also a trickster whose bad behavior often caused many problems. In some regions, Nanabozho is known as Winabojo or Nanabush.

Images depicting traditional stories can be found on Ojibwa baskets and other art.

PICTURES

Members of the Midewiwin Society used birch-bark scrolls to record myths and rules for ceremonies. These scrolls served as memory aids for the shamans who had to remember songs, rituals, and recipes for healing medicines. The Ojibwa writing system did not contain an alphabet. Instead, they used pictographs to record information. These symbolic pictures were scratched onto birch-bark sheets. Pictures included human and animal figures, spirits, and various shapes and patterns.

The Ojibwa sometimes drew pictures on rocks. They used ochre to draw or paint pictographs on rocks. Other times, pictures were carved onto rocks. These pictures are called petroglyphs.

Some petroglyphs represented dreams or visions of shamans and other Ojibwa people. For example, a young person on a vision quest might receive a dream name in his or her vision. This special name was never spoken out loud, but it could be recorded as a petroglyph.

Ojibwa Art

Art was part of everyday life for the Ojibwa. Clothing, tools, and ceremonial items were finely crafted.

Women decorated clothing, bags, baskets, and other objects with porcupine quills. Quills were plucked from a dead porcupine and sorted by size. The quills were dyed. Ojibwa women knew how to make bright dyes of blue, green, red, yellow, and black from local plants. Porcupine quills were used in a variety of ways. They could

The Ojibwa sewed beadwork on clothing items such as velvet vests.

be woven or braided. They could be wrapped around wooden handles and pipe stems. They could even be threaded to make jewelry and belts.

Beadwork was often sewn on items such as bags.

The Ojibwa were also skilled weavers. Craftspeople wove strips of bark to create mats and bags. Different shades of bark created interesting patterns in the weaving.

Ojibwa men were talented wood carvers. They created bowls, spoons, and other items. These pieces were often decorated with engraved figures.

Today, the Ojibwa still practice traditional arts and crafts. Many craftspeople earn their income by selling moccasins, clothing, baskets, jewelry, and other items. These objects often become valuable collectors' items.

BIRCH BARK

Birch-bark biting is a unique art form that has been practiced by the Ojibwa for hundreds of years. The artist selects a paper-thin piece of birch bark. The bark cannot have holes or marks. The artist carefully folds the birch bark. The artist uses his or her fingernail to scratch a design onto the folded bark. Then, the artist uses his or her canine, or pointed teeth, to bite into the bark and trace the design. The tooth marks leave a delicate pattern when the bark is unfolded.

The Ojibwa made birch-bark containers by heating the bark over a fire until it could be easily bent into a specific shape.

Ojibwa Creation

According to Ojibwa oral history, the world began with Mother Earth, Father Sky, Grandmother Moon, and Grandfather Sun. The Great Spirit took the four elements of earth, wind, fire, and water from Mother Earth. Using a sacred shell, the Great Spirit blew the breath of life into these elements. He created the first man, Nanabozho. The Great Spirit lowered Nanabozho to Earth.

Another story tells how the Ojibwa came to live around the Great Lakes. The story began with the Great Spirit sending a crane to make its home on Earth. As it flew toward Earth, the bird gave a loud, echoing cry. The crane circled around the Great Lakes and let out a second cry. The crane was pleased with the clear water and many fish in the lakes. It decided to live on the Great Lakes. Again, it gave a loud, echoing cry. The people of the Bear Clan, Catfish Clan, Marten Clan, and Loon Clan heard the crane's call and gathered on the shores of the Great Lakes.

The crane or heron is very important to the Ojibwa. The crane represents a position of influence. It is also a clan symbol, and members of this clan traditionally are speakers at meetings.

MODERN ARTIST

Sam English

Sam English is an Ojibwa painter and community activist. He is a member of the Turtle Mountain Chippewa Band of North Dakota. English studied architectural drafting and business, but he has always loved making art. He lives and works in Albuquerque, New Mexico.

English uses oil paints and gouache, a water-based paint. He paints long, elegant shapes in bold colors. His paintings feature American Indians in traditional dress and traditional settings. Some paintings include modern elements, too. Many of his works feature night skies with bright stars. The themes of English's works are American Indian pride and wellness. Art

has been a way for English to explore his own Native identity. He uses traditional symbols, such as the circle and the eagle, to represent love and strength. English describes his work as "inter-tribal"—all American Indians can share it.

English's work hangs in galleries and collections around the world. He has won numerous awards and commissions. The Presidential Inaugural Committee asked him to paint a mural for the 1997 Inauguration. English's

paintings have also been reproduced on posters and calendars.

English is committed to helping American Indians. He is a co-founder of the American Indian Youth Council. He often donates his artwork to organizations dedicated to Native American causes. English has been a guest speaker at several events promoting American Indian wellness and self-esteem.

Sam English runs his own gallery and studio in Albuquerque.

Studying the Ojibwa's Past

Archaeologists learn about the past by studying ancient artifacts. They have learned how the Ojibwa lived long ago by studying the sites of ancient villages. Archaeologists dig up the dirt at these sites in search of tools, weapons, food remains, and other objects. These items tell archaeologists how the Ojibwa hunted and fought. These items also help archaeologists understand traditional Ojibwa culture.

Oral histories are an important source of information about Ojibwa culture. These stories and legends are passed down from generation to generation. Ojibwa elders tell stories about traditional ways of life and past events. Elders help archaeologists understand pictographs and petroglyphs.

Recorded history also provides information about the Ojibwa's past. European explorers and traders observed Ojibwa culture. They recorded their observations. These records describe Ojibwa culture in the 1600s, when the Ojibwa first had contact with Europeans.

Decorating bark with quills is an ancient art. The Ojibwa have been decorating bark with quills for thousands of years.

TIME LINE

Archaic Period
Early Archaic Period
8000 B.C. – 6000 B.C.
Early American Indians settle around the Great Lakes.

Middle Archaic Period
6000 B.C. – 3000 B.C.
The Ojibwa settle around Lake Ojibwa, Wisconsin.

Late Archaic Period
3000 B.C. – 1000 B.C.
A burial site is created in Michigan's Upper Peninsula. It is discovered in 1994 by a construction crew.

Woodland Period
Early Woodland Period
1000 B.C. – 300 B.C.
American Indians use nets to fish in the Great Lakes.

Middle Woodland Period
300 B.C. – A.D. 500
Mound Builder Peoples live in the Upper Great Lakes region.

Late Woodland Period
A.D. 500 – 1620
The Ojibwa move from the east coast to the Great Lakes region.

Historic Period
French Period
1620 – 1763
France controls the Great Lakes region. The Ojibwa meet European traders, and missionaries. In 1660, the Ojibwa move west, into the Mississippi Valley.

British Period
1763 – 1814
Great Britain gains control of the Upper Great Lakes. An Ojibwa warrior named Pontiac leads a rebellion against the British.

American Period
1814 – present
The United States controls the Great Lakes region south of the Canadian border. The Ojibwa sign a series of treaties with the U.S. government. The Ojibwa are promised land, but some of the treaties are not honored. Reservations are established in Michigan, Minnesota, and Wisconsin.

Birch-bark Biting with Wax Paper

This activity allows you to try the ancient Ojibwa craft of birch-bark biting without having to hunt for a perfect piece of birch bark.

1. Cut a square of wax paper about 4 inches by 4 inches (10 centimeters by 10 centimeters).

2. Fold the wax paper in half diagonally, making a triangle.

3. Fold the triangle in half along the center line, making a smaller triangle.

4. With your fingernail, scratch a design onto the wax paper triangle. Traditional Ojibwa designs included animals, birds, flowers, insects, and leaves. You can create your own design.

5. Use your canine teeth to bite into the wax paper, following along the design you traced with your fingernail. You do not have to bite right through the wax paper–just leave a mark. Make your design interesting by changing the pressure of your bites. Try varying the space between your bites.

6. Unfold the wax paper to see the design you have made.

Further Reading

The following books about American Indians offer a great deal of information about the Ojibwa and other American Indian groups.

For an accurate account of traditional Ojibwa life, see *The American Indian* by Colin F. Taylor, Courage Books, 2002. Color and black and white photographs and illustrations show the traditional clothing, crafts, and homes of the Ojibwa.

A Native American Encyclopedia by Barry Pritzker, Oxford University Press, 2000, features an article about the Anishinaabe. This informative article discusses the history, traditions, culture, and contemporary life of the Ojibwa.

Web Sites

Learn more about the Ojibwa language at:
www.first-ojibwe.net/translations

Learn more about the American Indian Movement (AIM) at:
www.aimovement.org

Learn about the ancient history of the Ojibwa at:
www.cvmuseum.com/Paths1.html

Learn more about an Ojibwa community at:
www.ojibwa.com

GLOSSARY

archaeologists: scientists who study objects from the past to learn about past civilizations

artifacts: objects made by humans

awls: sharp, pointed tools for punching holes in leather

bands: groups of people who were related through marriage

bountiful: plentiful or abundant

buckskin: leather made from deerskin

clan: a group of families that were blood relatives

crane: a large wading bird with a long neck, long legs, and a long bill

dialects: changes in a language that is spoken in a certain place

environment: the area in which something exists or lives

language family: a group of languages that share similar origin, grammar, and words

migrated: moved from one region to another in a large group

mythology: a set of traditional stories about ancient times or natural events

powwows: American Indian events that feature traditional music, dancing, and singing

rawhide: untanned animal skin that has been allowed to harden

reprimanded: severely punished

reservations: lands set apart by the federal government for a special purpose, especially for the use by an American Indian group

rush mats: mats made from branches bull rush

sage: a plant with grayish-green leaves that is often used to flavor food

semi-nomadic: spending part of the year moving from place to place in search of animals to hunt

shamans: people with special spiritual powers

snares: traps that have a rope that tightens around small animals

tanned: animal hides made into leather

totem: an animal, plant, or natural object used as a symbol by American Indian clans

treaties: formal agreements between groups of people

INDEX